Chinese Modern New Technology Series

Mobile Payment

Edited by Li Chaodong

Translated by Xuemeng Angela Li

河海大學出版社
HOHAI UNIVERSITY PRESS

ROYAL COLLINS
Books Beyond Boundaries

Newsstand
Cash Payment
In our daily lives, we need to make payments when we buy things or make any other types of purchases.

Mobile Payment
Check-out
Card Payment
Nowadays, people make payments in various ways, so, how did the ancient people pay?

In the beginning, currency didn't exist in the ancient society. So, how did people make purchases?

People took out their prey and fruits for exchange with others to get what they needed in return. This is the so-called "barter exchange."

For example, if the person who has a goat needs fruits and the person who owns fruits happens to want a goat, then they can successfully exchange with each other. However, if the person with fruit wants grains instead, then more exchanges will be needed for each person to get what they need, making it a very complicated process.

As a result, people start to seek media for exchange, of which the value can be recognized by everyone—a "universal equivalent."

Animals like cows and goats are not ideal choices because they are difficult to divide and carry.

Therefore, seashells have become the first currency for their difficulty of accessibility, high value, and small size, which makes them easy to count and carry.

With increasingly frequent exchanges, the limited quantity of seashells can no longer meet people's demands as a currency.

During the Shang and Zhou dynasties (1600–256 BC), the technology of bronze smelting went through rapid development. People started to use metal elements from nature to copy seashells, which marked the birth of bronze coins.

During the Warring States period (475–221 BC), each state manufactured its own bronze coin due to the competition between feudal lords.

These bronze coins have diverse styles and weights and cannot be recognized by every state, making it difficult for people to make payments when they visit other states.

Yan
Zhao
Qi
Wei
Han
Chu
Qin

Coin Casting

After Qin Shi Huang (First Qin Emperor, 259–210 BC) conquered the six states, he unified the state currencies to facilitate commodity transactions. The new currency is round with a square hole in the center. It weighs about half a tael of bronze and is thus named "Qin Half Tael."

Qin "Half Tael"

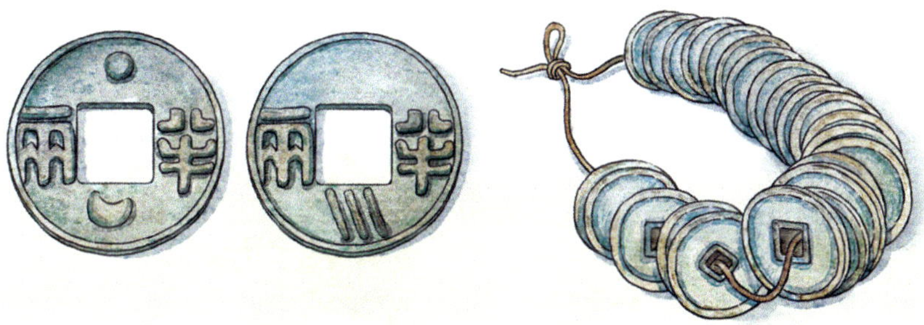

The coin design of a round shape and a square hole is cost-saving and portable. It also ingeniously caters to the ancient concept of the universe, "The dome-liked sky covers the square earth," and has been continuously adopted in later dynasties.

Han "Wuzhu"
(It means the weight of five *zhu*, a weight unit of Han.)

Tang "Kai Yuan Tong Bao"
(It means a new, better life.)

But bronze coins are too heavy to carry around. During the Song Dynasty (960–1279), the business sector became tremendously prosperous, where money was frequently used. The first paper money Jiaozi thus came out. China has also become the first country in the world to adopt paper money.

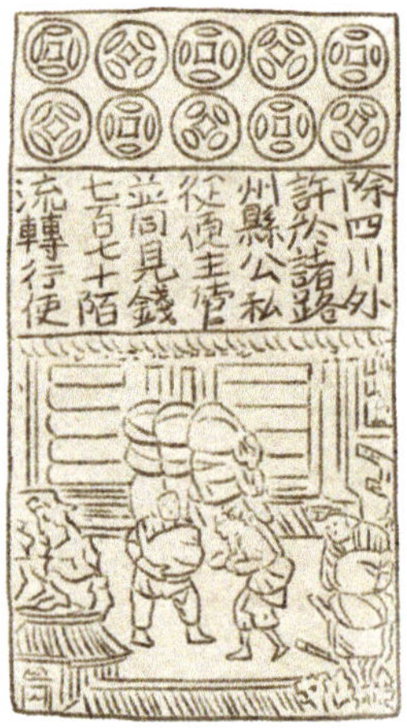

The administration of the Yuan Dynasty (1271–1368) actively promoted the use of paper money, making it the sole fiat money at the time. When Marco Polo (1254–1324) visited China from the West, he was also amazed by Yuan's practice of assigning value to paper money.

Due to the huge convenience of issuing paper money, the administration printed new notes whenever it ran out of budget.

Large sums of paper money flew into the private sector and caused inflation and devaluation.*

During the Ming Dynasty (1368–1644), large amounts of silver from Japan and America entered the Chinese market due to the booming overseas trade activities. Silver sycee has become the main currency in Chinese people's daily life.

* Inflation is when prices go up over time, and devaluation is when a currency becomes less valuable compared to others.

Silver Sycee of Ming Dynasty

Money is a great invention of mankind as a means of payment. The emergence of *piaohao* (draft bank), where exchange and deposit services of gold and silver are offered to people, has brought new changes to the business sector.

During the Ming and Qing dynasties (1368–1911), long-distance trade activities developed rapidly. Merchants carried large amounts of silver through long travels, bearing great risk to buy and sell goods, which led to the establishment of *piaohao*.

After merchants deposit their silver sycee in *piaohao*, the institute will draw a bill of exchange and then tear it in half. The merchant and the institute each take half as a copy. When merchants need more money, they can take half of the bill of exchange to *piaohao* for withdrawal. At the time, the famous Shanxi *piaohao* had franchises all over China, with the farthest even reaching Russia.

匯通天下
日昇昌記

Qianzhuang and *piaohao* both functioned as banks throughout Chinese history by operating exchange and deposit services.

However, the first official bank in China was not founded until the end of the Opium Wars (1839–1860)* when Guangdong and Shanghai subsequently opened up as ports.

* The Opium Wars were two aggressive wars launched by Western powers against China in the mid-19th century.

With Britain, the United States, France, Germany, Russia, and other countries setting up banks in China, a large number of foreign currencies were circulating in the Chinese market. By the 1930s, the negative consequences of chaotic currencies had permeated the daily lives of Chinese people. The economic crisis of foreign countries also spread to China. Although the national government carried out a variety of reforms, it failed to stop the rising prices.

After the establishment of the People's Republic of China, the situation was finally reversed.

The government undertook financial reforms.

The outbreak of economic crises caused protests.

Finance Department

After the People's Republic of China was founded, China was in a transitional stage where thousands of national causes needed to be developed. The original monetary and financial systems both require rebuilding. At that time, due to the rocket-high price of grain, salt, and medicine, the administration came up with the measure of paying grains instead of money and salary so that the subsistent lives of people could be guaranteed.

Later, during the planned economy era, the state issued a fixed number of food, clothing, and other coupons based on the population. Coupons have become the key payment method for people's purchases.

In the 1940s, the renminbi (RMB) issued by the People's Bank of China officially became China's fiat money. Since it is endorsed by national credit, a hundred *yuan* RMB note can be exchanged for items of a hundred *yuan* value, even though the note itself costs much less to make.

ople's Bank of China

However, the inconvenience of carrying large amounts of cash is often distressing when people travel. The creation of bank cards relieved such concern.

When people deposit their money in the bank, the bank issues a card as proof. To complete a purchase, it only takes a swipe of the card to notify the bank about the transaction and deduct money from the account accordingly.

After the reform and opening up, China learned from the industry experience of foreign bank cards and rapidly expanded its bank card businesses by applying electronic computers. In 2002, with the approval of the State Council and the People's Bank of China, all the major commercial banks and institutions united to establish China UnionPay. The money that people deposited in different banks can now be transferred across banks, which achieved the goal of "one card in hand to travel across China" in reality.

But what if the card has run out of money? Don't worry; a credit card was thus created for us to complete the purchase first and pay the bill later.

Credit cards originated in the United States. It is a card that endorses the cardholder's identity and financial capability and allows the cardholder to purchase with credits. This new way of payment is built on the validity of personal credit. It has changed the old payment ideal of "cash on delivery" and reformed the payment sector.

Credit card payment requires a credit card machine to complete.

But not every merchant is capable of running one. Switching between different bank cards has also created new inconveniences for the users.

Therefore, a new payment method was born—mobile payment.

Once we connect our phone with our bank cards, we can complete purchases simply by scanning the payment QR code. Mobile payment helps us to get rid of changes and wait times. On top of that, no more switching between cards is necessary, which precisely presents the convenience of mobile payment.

However, the "scan to pay" function has also led to certain financial safety risks, such as identity theft. Payment also cannot be completed when the phone is out of battery.

Payment methods have been transforming in new directions, including facial recognition and fingerprints. This is because biometric information uniquely belongs to everyone. These new biometric payment methods have been gradually changing our daily lives.

China's mobile payment technology is undoubtedly leading across the world. It is characterized by faster development, higher usage, and a wider network. Nowadays, Chinese people can basically live a cashless life by paying with their phones and QR codes.

The Forecasting of the Chinese Digital Payment Transaction Scale

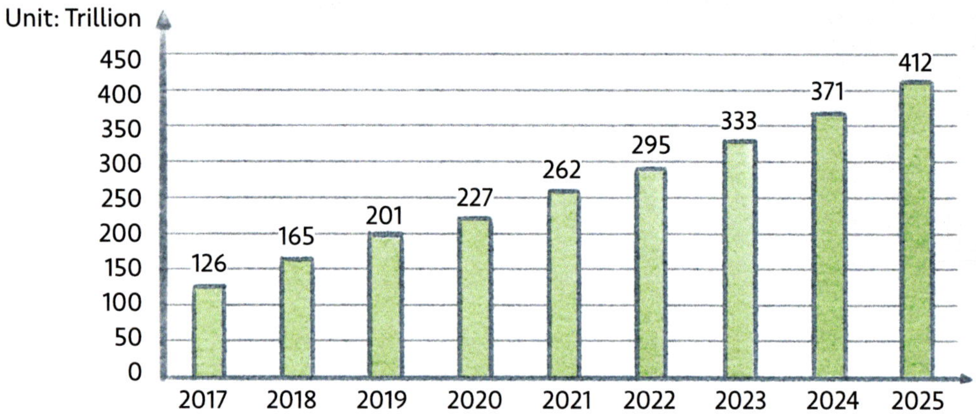

The Proportion of Digital Payment Market Size by Region in 2020

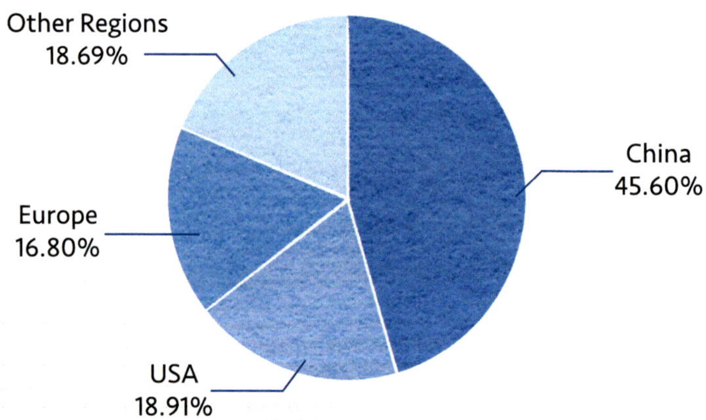

With the rapid development of new information technologies, such as big data and 5G, the future scale of mobile payment in China will continuously expand with increasingly diverse forms.

Convenience Store
Convenience Store
The essential function of money as the equivalent of exchange has never changed. It is the form and method of payment that kept changing.
The future of mobile payment is so unpredictable!

Chinese Modern New Technology Series
Mobile Payment

Edited by Li Chaodong
Translated by Xuemeng Angela Li

First published in 2024 by Royal Collins Publishing Group Inc.
Groupe Publication Royal Collins Inc.
550-555 boul. René-Lévesque O Montréal (Québec) H2Z1B1 Canada

ISBN: 978-1-4878-1239-3